W9-APY-796

Date: 4/26/17

J 536.078 POL
Polinsky, Paige V.,
Super simple experiments
with heat and cold : fun and

SUPER SIMPLE
SCIENCE AT WORK

SUPER SIMPLE
EXPERIMENTS
WITH
HEAT AND COLD

FUN AND INNOVATIVE SCIENCE PROJECTS

PAIGE V. POLINSKY

CONSULTING EDITOR, DIANE CRAIG, M.A./READING SPECIALIST

Super Sandcastle

An Imprint of Abdo Publishing
abdopublishing.com

abdopublishing.com

Published by Abdo Publishing, a division of ABDO, PO Box 398166, Minneapolis, Minnesota 55439. Copyright © 2017 by Abdo Consulting Group, Inc. International copyrights reserved in all countries. No part of this book may be reproduced in any form without written permission from the publisher. Super SandCastle™ is a trademark and logo of Abdo Publishing.

Printed in the United States of America, North Mankato, Minnesota
062016
092016

THIS BOOK CONTAINS
RECYCLED MATERIALS

Editor: Liz Salzmann
Content Developer: Nancy Tuminelly
Cover and Interior Design and Production: Mighty Media, Inc.
Photo Credits: Mighty Media, Inc.; Shutterstock; Wikimedia Commons

The following manufacturers/names appearing in this book are trademarks: Learning Resources®

Library of Congress Cataloging-in-Publication Data

Names: Polinsky, Paige V., author.
Title: Super simple experiments with heat and cold : fun and innovative
    science projects / Paige V. Polinsky ; consulting editor, Diane Craig,
    M.A./reading specialist.
Description: Minneapolis, Minnesota : Abdo Publishing, [2017] |
    Series: Super simple science at work
Identifiers: LCCN 2016006222 (print) | LCCN 2016017134 (ebook) | ISBN
    9781680781700 (print) | ISBN 9781680776133 (ebook)
Subjects: LCSH: Heat--Experiments--Juvenile literature. | Temperature
    measurements--Juvenile literature. | Science--Experiments--Juvenile
    literature. | Science projects--Juvenile literature.
Classification: LCC QC320.14 .P65 2016 (print) | LCC QC320.14 (ebook) | DDC
    536.078--dc23
LC record available at https://lccn.loc.gov/2016006222

Super SandCastle™ books are created by a team of professional educators, reading specialists, and content developers around five essential components—phonemic awareness, phonics, vocabulary, text comprehension, and fluency—to assist young readers as they develop reading skills and strategies and increase their general knowledge. All books are written, reviewed, and leveled for guided reading and early reading intervention programs for use in shared, guided, and independent reading and writing activities to support a balanced approach to literacy instruction.

To Adult Helpers

The projects in this title are fun and simple. There are just a few things to remember to keep kids safe. Some projects require the use of sharp or hot objects. Also, kids may be using messy materials such as glue or paint. Make sure they protect their clothes and work surfaces. Review the projects before starting, and be ready to assist when necessary.

KEY SYMBOLS

Watch for these warning symbols in this book. Here is what they mean.

HOT!
You will be working with something hot. Get help!

SHARP!
You will be working with a sharp object. Get help!

CONTENTS

HEAT ENERGY
AT WORK

Have you ever sat near a campfire? Could you feel its heat? Touch your forehead. People give off heat too!

Heat is a type of energy. Every **substance** contains this type of energy. The more heat energy something has, the higher its temperature.

SNOW HAS LITTLE HEAT ENERGY.

FIRE HAS A LOT OF HEAT ENERGY.

ATOMS & MOLECULES

Heat is created by the movement of atoms. Atoms are very small. Everything is made of atoms. Atoms can bond together. Bonded atoms form **molecules**. Hydrogen and oxygen atoms bond to form water.

Atoms and molecules are always moving. They move faster when heat energy is added. The temperature of the **substance** rises. Removing heat energy slows the atoms and molecules down. The temperature of the substance lowers.

WATER MOLECULE

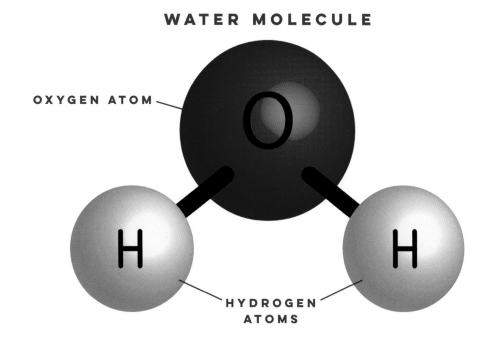

OXYGEN ATOM

O

H   H

HYDROGEN
ATOMS

MEASURING
TEMPERATURE

An object's temperature is how hot or cold it is. We use thermometers to measure temperature.

Temperature is measured in **degrees**. Water boils at 212 degrees Fahrenheit (100°C). Water freezes at 32 degrees Fahrenheit (0°C).

BOILING WATER

FROZEN WATER

TEMPERATURE SCALES

There are several temperature scales. Fahrenheit (°F) and Celsius (°C) are the two main scales. The Fahrenheit scale is used most often in the United States. The Celsius scale is used in countries that use the **metric** system.

WORK LIKE
A SCIENTIST

You've learned about temperature. Now you're ready to experiment! Scientists have a special way of working. It is called the Scientific Method. Follow the steps to work like a scientist. It's super simple!

THE SCIENTIFIC METHOD

Have a notebook and pencil handy. Scientists write down everything that happens in their experiments. They also write down their thoughts and ideas.

1. QUESTION

What question are you trying to answer? Write down your question. Then do some **research** to find out more about it.

2. GUESS

Try to guess the answer to your question. Write down your guess.

ANDERS CELSIUS

Anders Celsius was an astronomer. He invented the centigrade temperature scale. Until that time, people measured temperature in many different ways. Celsius wanted there to be a standard way. Using the same scale helped scientists compare results of their experiments. The centigrade scale was later renamed after Celsius.

3. EXPERIMENT

Create an experiment to help answer your question. Write down the steps. Make a list of the supplies you'll need. Then do the experiment. Write down what happens.

4. ANALYSIS

Study the results of your experiment. Did it answer your question? Was your guess correct?

5. CONCLUSION

Think about how the experiment went. Why was your guess wrong or right? Write down the reasons.

MATERIALS

Here are some of the materials that you will need for the experiments in this book.

AEROSOL HAIR SPRAY

BALLOONS

CLAY OR PLAY DOUGH

CLEAR TAPE

CONSTRUCTION PAPER

DRINKING GLASS

DRINKING STRAWS

EFFERVESCENT TABLETS

FOOD COLORING

HAMMER

ICE CUBES

KETTLE

LARGE NAIL

MARKER

MASON JAR
WITH LID

MEASURING CUP

METAL SPOON

MUGS

OVEN MITT

PENCIL

PITCHER

PLASTIC BOTTLE

PLASTIC SPOON

RUBBING ALCOHOL

SAUCEPAN

SCRAP WOOD

STOPWATCH

THERMOMETER

WATER

WOODEN SPOON

DIY
THERMOMETER

MATERIALS: mason jar with lid, water, rubbing alcohol, measuring cups, red food coloring, scrap wood, marker, hammer, large nail, drinking straw, clay or play dough

Some thermometers have the temperature scale marked on the outside. They have a liquid inside. The liquid **expands** or contracts depending on its temperature. The liquid moves to a number on the scale to show the temperature.

MAKE A LIQUID THERMOMETER!

① Put equal amounts of rubbing alcohol and water in the jar. Together, they should fill the jar one-quarter full.

② Add a few drops of food coloring.

③ Screw the lid on the jar. Shake it up!

④ Remove the lid. Put the center of the lid on a piece of scrap wood. Mark the center of the lid.

⑤ Carefully hammer the nail through the mark. Make a hole big enough for the drinking straw.

⑥ Put the lid back on the jar.

Continued on the next page.

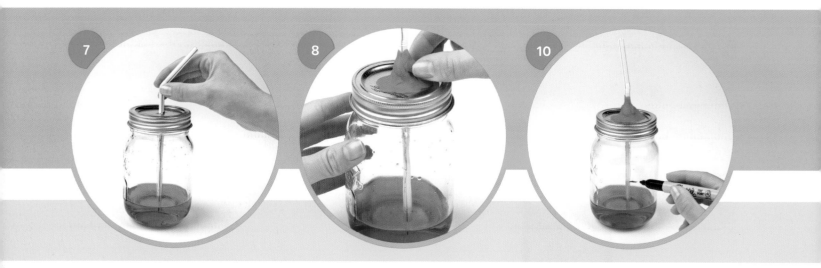

DIY THERMOMETER (CONTINUED)

7 Push the straw through the hole until it touches the liquid. Do not let the straw touch the bottom of the jar.

8 Pack clay around the straw. Make sure the hole is sealed.

9 Place the jar in the sun for 2 hours.

10 Draw a line even with the water level in the straw.

11 Put the jar in the shade for 2 hours.

12 Draw a line even with the water level in the straw. Is this line above or below the first line you drew?

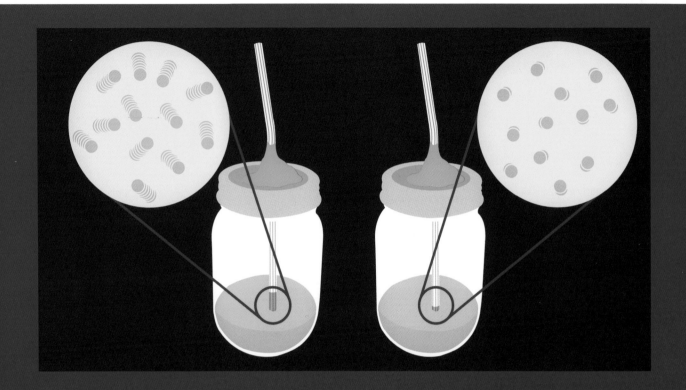

WHY IT WORKS

The more heat energy something has, the more its atoms move. The atoms take up more space as they move. When atoms move less, they take up less space. When the jar is in the sun, the liquid gains heat energy. The atoms move more. So the liquid **expands**, moving up the straw. The liquid loses heat energy when the jar is in the shade. The liquid contracts and moves down the straw.

COLOR CUPS

MATERIALS: 3 drinking glasses, water, 3 thermometers, construction paper (black, orange & white), clear tape, timer

All things need light in order to be visible. The sun is one source of light. Sunlight is made up of seven colors. Objects **absorb** or reflect these colors. The colors an object absorbs affect its temperature.

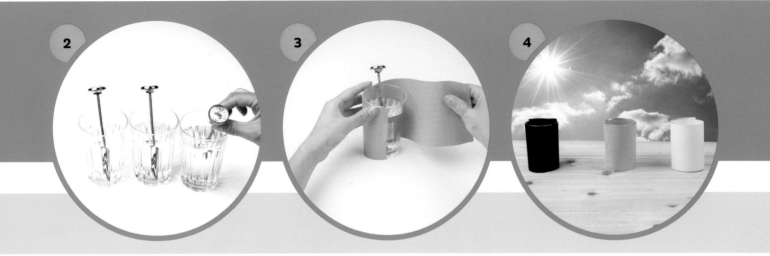

WATCH COLOR AFFECT TEMPERATURE!

① Fill the glasses with room temperature water.

② Use thermometers to measure the water's starting temperature. The water in all three glasses should be the same temperature.

③ Tape construction paper around the glasses. Use a different color for each glass.

④ Place the glasses in a sunny spot. Be sure they all receive an equal amount of sunlight. Leave the glasses in the sun for 1 hour.

Continued on the next page.

COLOR CUPS (CONTINUED)

⑤ Place the thermometers back in the glasses. Wait 1 minute.

⑥ Check each thermometer's temperature again.

⑦ The water in the white glass should be about the same as the starting temperature. The water in the orange glass should be slightly warmer than the white glass. The water in the black glass should be the warmest.

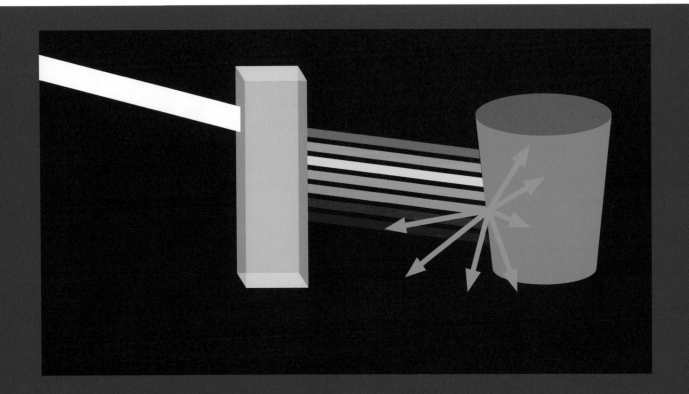

WHY IT WORKS

The colors in sunlight are red, orange, yellow, green, blue, indigo, and violet. When sunlight hits an object, the object may **absorb** all of these colors. This makes the object look black. If the object absorbs none of the colors, it looks white. If an object absorbs all but one color, it will look that color. Light is made up of energy. The more colors an object absorbs, the more light energy it receives. This is why the sun warms the water in the black cup the most!

SPOON CONDUCTION

MATERIALS: saucepan, water, oven mitts, 4 mugs, wooden spoon, plastic spoon, metal spoon, 3 thermometers, timer

Atoms move more when they get warm. When a warm object touches another object, the movement gets passed to the second object. It warms up. This type of heat **transfer** is called conduction.

WHY IT WORKS

The hot water passes heat to the spoons. Then the spoons pass heat to the water in the other mugs. But some **substances** don't conduct as well as others. How much heat transfers depends on how close together the **molecules** are.

The molecules in metal are packed tightly together. They easily pass their movement to things they touch. This is why the metal spoon heats the water more than the wooden or plastic spoons do. The molecules in wood and plastic are farther apart. So, they transfer less heat.

TRANSFER HEAT ENERGY WITH WATER!

① Boil water in the saucepan. Carefully pour some of the water into a mug.

② Place all three spoons in the mug.

③ Fill three mugs with cold water. Put a thermometer in each mug. Make sure they are all the same temperature.

④ Move each spoon from the hot mug to one of the other mugs.

⑤ Wait 5 minutes. Then compare the temperatures. The mug with the metal spoon should have the hottest water.

TABLET
RACE

MATERIALS: 2 mason jars, hot tap water, cold water, red & blue food coloring, 2 effervescent tablets, stopwatch, notebook, pencil

A chemical **reaction** happens when atoms and **molecules** interact and **rearrange**. How fast this occurs is the rate of reaction. Since temperature affects how fast molecules move, it affects reaction time.

TIME TABLETS AT TWO TEMPERATURES!

1 Fill one jar with cold water. Add a few drops of blue food coloring.

2 Fill the second jar with hot tap water. Add a few drops of red food coloring.

3 Drop a tablet into the jar that has red food coloring. Start the stopwatch.

Continued on the next page.

TABLET RACE (CONTINUED)

4 Stop the stopwatch when the tablet is gone. Write down the time it took for it to disappear.

5 Repeat steps 3 and 4 with the jar that has blue food coloring.

6 Compare the times. Did the tablet disappear faster in the blue jar or the red jar?

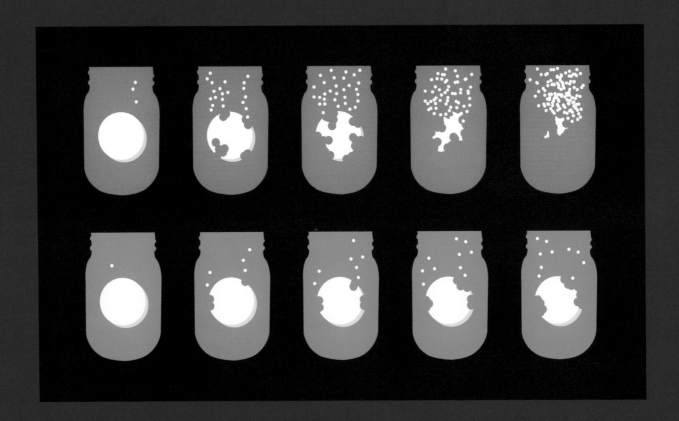

WHY IT WORKS

When the tablet touches the water, a chemical **reaction** occurs. The atoms in the tablet begin to rearrange and **fizz**. Atoms move more quickly when they are warm. That's why the reaction happens more quickly in the hot water.

BALLOON
BLOWUP

MATERIALS: balloon, plastic bottle, timer, hot tap water, pitcher

Density is how close together something's **molecules** are. Gases, such as air, are not very dense. Their molecules are spread far apart. Temperature affects how close molecules are to each other. This can cause matter to **expand** or contract.

WHY IT WORKS

In the freezer, the air in the bottle becomes denser. The molecules move closer together. The air takes up less space, so it sucks the balloon toward the bottle. The hot water warms the air in the bottle. So, the molecules move farther apart. The air needs more space, so it pushes into the balloon!

MOVE MOLECULES WITH HEAT!

1 Stretch the balloon over the top of the bottle.

2 Place the bottle in the freezer. Wait 15 minutes.

3 Fill the pitcher with hot tap water.

4 Remove the bottle from the freezer. What happened to the balloon?

5 Put the bottle in the pitcher. Make sure the water covers the bottle's sides. The balloon should start to fill with air!

CLOUD JAR

MATERIALS: water, kettle, mason jar with lid, ruler, food coloring, oven mitt, ice cubes, timer, aerosol hair spray

There are three main forms of matter. They are solids, liquids, and gases. Temperature can cause matter to change form. Heat turns solids into liquids and liquids into gases. Cold turns liquids and gases into solids.

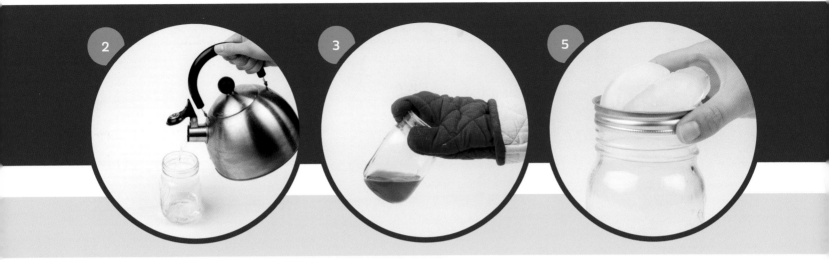

CREATE AN ARTIFICIAL CLOUD!

① Fill the kettle with water. Bring the water to a boil.

② Pour about 1 inch (2.5 cm) of hot water into the jar. Add a few drops of food coloring.

③ Put on the oven mitt. Pick up the jar and swish the hot water around. Make sure the water touches the sides of the jar.

④ Turn the lid upside down. Lay it on top of the jar.

⑤ Place a few ice cubes on top of the lid. Wait about 20 seconds.

Continued on the next page.

CLOUD JAR (CONTINUED)

6 Remove the lid. Quickly spray hair spray into the jar.

7 Put the lid and ice back on as fast as you can. Observe the jar. A cloud should form.

8 When you can see the cloud clearly, remove the lid. Watch the cloud drift out of the jar!